Best Wishes

Neil Paston

Here,
   I gather up
   my fragmented self –
   bind it together
   with a thought –
   and settle down
   to be.

*With all things living
    we share one common place,
    one common bond.
We are on the growing edge
    of life.*

On The Growing Edge

Text and Photographs
by
Philip Rusten

Lithographed in The United States of America by

Tecumseh Printers
Tecumseh, Michigan

I am only once.
I am no other time.
  The quest
  must be here,
  must be now –
for I am no other time.

Preface

One October morning, so many years ago, I flew with a friend over a woods where yesterday's late sun had warmed my back—propped as I was against a small maple sapling. How microscopic my view had been, riveted on a knothole high up in a white oak where a grey squirrel watched me with an equal intentness!

Now it was macroscopic. Woods stretched onto woods. Checkerboarding fields where men spent their entire lives, surrounded towns that chronicled generations of family living. My eye stretched beyond the farmlands and villages along the Wisconsin River that centuries ago had carried the French fur traders as it made its winding way over shifting sand bars to merge in a wide delta with the grandest of all rivers—the mighty Mississippi.

Was I better for this exalted view? Did its grandeur invalidate yesterday's fixation on a single knothole in a single white oak in order to gain a single glance at one solitary grey squirrel? I know better. Seeing is seeing. Understanding is understanding—be it of squirrels or of planets. I hunger for both. Each in its own way gives me life and joy.

To see is to be—whether the seeing is a new view or an old understanding. Through the eyes of sight or the eyes of thought the world pours in and we become who we are.

During my first hectic week of college, someone said, "We are what we think about all day." It scared me. My thoughts then—as now—could hardly bear such close scrutiny! Even though the years have confirmed this simple wisdom, I am not now afraid. I am wiser. I know I can also add or subtract from that awful judgment just by what I "see." New experiences, new ideas, let me grow beyond my limitations. I am transformed, enlarged, in such dramatic ways by such simple things—a butterfly wing, a wink from a friend, a sudden fear, a hill-top view.

This book is a sharing of those enlargements. Some are very old. Others are as new as the words on this page. What a delight it is to recall, to remember—sift and ponder—the seeings that have been, and are, the growing edge of my life. Perhaps some of them will send you on a journey of your own as full of pleasant wanderings and joy as these have been for me.

Phil Rusten

The quest for being
is a quest, not a possession.
It is in what we ARE doing,
not in what we have done.

In Creativity

Thoughtfingers
        unlocking
            mind doors
       releasing
           the ineffable
       shaping
          wispy thought

dance across   space,
        white   myself in hot pursuit.

I
who
tumble about
inside my body
seeking escape through eyes
            voice
            hands
am born on paper
birthed
     by a finger-cradled pencil.

The Creative Eye

The sun isn't visible in the pre-dawn darkness, but it is there. My waking body knew it long before my eyes had enough light with which to function. It responded to the beginning day, prodding me out of bed into semi-awareness. Beyond the window a foreboding coldness and isolation suggested that this was a bad decision. The huge walnut tree, behind which the sun would soon emerge, seemed to be a street-corner derelict—cold, lost, friendless. It was just my eyes again, playing tricks with memories of other mornings, other scenes, other places. It takes such a minute fragment of thought, such a tiny bit of sight to unlock the lifetime my eyes have saved and filed away. I often wonder what I really know, what visions of the past are yet to be remembered, perhaps understood, for the first time. It might be that some dawn I will look out a different window in a different direction and my eyes will trigger a new visual print-out, a composite one, re-arranging things in a fresh and life-giving way. I will call it "creativity," but it will be just my eyes again, playing tricks.

The sun is above the horizon now and the skim of morning clouds has a golden edge to it. The fog is reddish blue and the maze of houses and winter trees seem spectral, empty. There is a touch of optimism in the pale blue sky-space, conveying that gentle urgency morning always brings. I am buoyed up by all of this and the day begins to take shape, seeming more possible, more desirable than that dimly silhouetted world into which I first stepped just before dawn.

Some mornings, visual imagery not from the eye—the memory of hurt or weakness—fear-built images flitting about behind the eye—intrude to gloom the dawn, darkening, shadowing. At best, then, I am schizophrenic, half sun, half shadow. There is no dawn, no

Country Morn

growing light, only hurt and fear and hate. Then it is that my eyes reach out to find a cleansing and a healing. They seek the sun-made dawn and sweep away the fear-built morning.

The sun IS coming up. It started there behind the grove of winter trees and stretched slowly into fullness and roundness, losing that illusion of flatness as it crested the horizon. Now, as it edges over the top of the trees, I can actually see the sun move upward. It almost seems to roll out of the earth. My early impatience gives way to wonder and enchantment.

The sky has changed to that "winter morning grey-blue" and I've changed, too, growing more accepting of the inevitable routine dailyness with its tedium I had wistfully thought I could avoid as dawn first broke over the houses. I am glad for that deceptive moment in the dawn, though. I am richer for it and life is more possible. It was my eyes. They did it, responding to shape and shadow, to color and brightness. They couldn't resist. Their weakness—their vulnerability—is my benefactor and I am grateful. I shall reward them with many early mornings and let them play their little game with me as often as they will.

A teasing thought
came from between the words.
I wandered after it
to become friends.

Wild Geranium At Dawn

That Audacious Idea

An idea came scattering,
my contentment,
chaosing the moment.
It took no notice.
of the NO TREPASSING sign
placed prominently
over the threshold
of my mind.

It moved right in,
set up its easel,
began to sketch
what ought to be.

Its penciled noises
disintegrated my isolation;
evaporated my complacency.

Some ideas
are like that —
                audacious,
                irreverent.

Impudent lives they lead!
So upsetting they are
                . . .to pre-ordained order.

In The Quiet Places

Sunning, Mostly...

There are no grey days that cannot be scrubbed bright by happy thoughts! An inner sun glows the edges of leaves or of a friend's hair with a brightness as real as that bestowed by a sunrise. My happy thoughts are not contrived. They are—and therefore I am—inwardly bright and warm. I feel like a squirrel perched on a stub of a limb with no urge to be elsewhere. In my mind's eye I am that special grey squirrel I came to know each morning of the Fall—sitting, backed up to the tree trunk, scratching as the need struck, sunning mostly. His serenity, his inner health, is what I remember most— and envy. It seemed to have come to him so easily, so naturally. Mine has been so hard won.

I distrust "happy thoughts" that come at unlikely times in unlikely places. They court deception, play "Pollyanna" with my mind. They cannot be other than false.

The happy thoughts that cleansed my mind atop Mount Lander in the Wind River Range during the sudden hail-rain storm were understandable, therefore believable. I sat on the top rock viewing the northward expanse of the glaciers and time became geological. My humanness had a generation feel to it and my inevitable death a natural part of all that was and was to be. A glow emanated from my inner being that no fear, no failure, no depression could override. IT WAS, therefore I was!

We need such simple things! A daffodil . . . the touch of textured stone . . . the morning cardinal song from high atop the maple tree. . . . the sound of running water . . . the aroma of fresh earth, moist and mulched. Who is it among us that declares we are not earth-children? What robbers are they that try to steal our tree-made heritage from us . . . telling us "we are but strangers here"? Why do they want to deny us our closest link to life? Do they fear reality? Do they prefer ego-fantasies to the wonder of a shared universe? Why must we be "other-than" when it is such a joy to be "part-of"?

I touch the leaf with ecstasy. It gives me oxygen, and ultimately, fire-warmth. The crumbling leaf mould trickles through my fingers and I gently wonder at the life and the lives it took to make it. Tree branches creak, stretch to new dimensions, weaving shadow-patterns on the lawn beneath. Through storm and adversity, sunshine and snow, wars and triumphs, they weave and grow. They build my world and some say I should exclude them from my life by feeling superior? I am embarrassed.

My skills are my own. The tree cannot do what I can do—nor can I do what it can do. Does this not make us partners? I rejoice in that fact, lean back against its sturdy body, scratch as the need strikes, sunning, mostly.

Quietness opens the door
    inviting us out
    for a visual lunch.
The menu is never printed...
    the chefs always improvise!

Sanctuary

Sun patterns
  dance across
  the pages of my mind.
Their word shapes
  sketch warm and lovely
  thoughts....

The Fishermen

Mill Creek Morning

Quietness
is the presence
of harmony,
not the absence
of noise.

Where there is joy...
do not hurry.

Serenity

Wilderness Grasses

White Sands

The setting sun
lets us know
there is more to life
than we can see.

Jamaican Sunset

Beyond Boundaries

Above my head,
a fleecy cloud.
My mind, watching it,
travels a far journey.

A Better Way

I have secluded myself to write. It is silent, private, unchanging within these four walls. On this hiking trip I must provide my own sights, sounds and scenery. There is enough. My memory is full— and what is more, I can go from Mijinemungshing Lake in Ontario to the Wind River glaciers in Wyoming in a flick of mind cell! Hitching carefully chosen words to those flashing vignettes, slows them down enough so that I can chat with them before some newcomer intrudes. Fireside thinkers need time to make an acquaintance.

There is a three minute incident on a hiking trail above Peterson's Meadow on the eastern slope of the Wind River range. My mind walks around and around it, observing it from every angle, touching it here, adjusting it there to rouse it from its memory-sleep. Finally, it is possible to hear deep labored breathing, the squeak of boot leather and the stretching of the pack straps. Then from above comes the sounds of a pack train . . . Sunday fishermen returning from an overnight at Lost Lake and a "wilderness trip."

I stepped off the path to let them by. Resting against the tree was a welcomed respite. Stones rattled down the path and into the woods. The riders are visible now. Horses are huffing, riders rolling with the lurching body-twisting saddles, legs braced against the downward trip. First comes the guide, leading two pack mules— sleepy-eyed, scheming creatures with no illusions about "wilderness trips." Immediately behind is the boy, probably seventeen, and very protected from the wilderness. He is attired in parent-money, indulgently spent, a carbon copy of the three men rolling along behind him. Here is no seasoned veteran of the rugged outdoors. He has been deprived of struggle, sacrifice and hardship— the stuff of which youthful dreams are made.

I have been on the trail for only two days, but haven't shaven in fourteen. Sweat and my unconditioned legs complete my appearance. In this youth's eyes I must be some ancient mountain man going home to live once more with his faithful wolf-dog alongside an idyllic mountain stream abounding with fish and game. I'm so tired and my every breath so labored, the vision would not be hard for him to conjure up. He is alongside now, his horse and other companions completely forgotten. His face reveals his awe.

"How long have you been out?" His voice was timid.

What would you have replied? More than a question, it was a request: "Please be more of the wilderness than what I have just seen!" Like so many of our questions, his sought worlds of which he knew not enough to be able to question them.

I've always been genuinely proud of my answer. Some greater voice than mine used my lips to give substance to his dream of a better world. It is not often we rise to the occasion before the fact. Our re-writes and we-should-have-said's are always so genuinely profound, so strikingly appropriate.

"Oh, I dunno . . . three, four weeks maybe . . . I've forgotten . . . yeah, it's four weeks, I guess," I managed to mumble, mountain style.

His awe-expelled "Gee!" as he rocked by, and his backward call of friendship, "Have a good trip!" have warmed my heart the most of anything my memory gives me from that trip. The trail was even easier to climb now.

The strangest thing of all was that my own journey was now so complete I could hardly continue. I made it to the trout lake and beyond, floundering up other ridges to stand and look at least, from the mountaintop. Then I strode gratefully homeward—very conscious of the hallowed spot on the trail where that reverent "Gee" had been uttered. Perhaps when we are able to be a dream-giver, our lives are so filled that there is no room for more, nor is there any need for more.

Reality is made so much more of dreams than we ever suspect. Men watch boys play games and wonder if perhaps the boys are right and it IS possible to win every time. Families tell stories to weave legends that make them invincible for a moment. The morning is a dream, temporarily pushing aside yesterday's reality. We erase the smudge of failure with dream-tipped pencils to write our plans for tomorrow. We cannot sing, but we can listen to music. We cannot travel, but we book-walk over all the earth. It is a dream world and who wants it recited in cold mathematical absolutes?

"Oh . . . I dunno . . . three, four weeks maybe . . . I've forgotten . . ." is the better way.

Teton Range, Wyoming

Mt. Moran at Jenny Lake

Time Between The Snows

Between two mountain ridges in lower Alberta, Canada, there runs a saddle—almost like a dam—blocking two deep valleys, one to the east, the other to the west. The conifers on the westward slope of that saddle, at its very peak, grow eastward—their tops no more than 15° from horizontal. Being new at things like this, Eric and I called them ground cedars and gave them no thought. Then we saw them as trees! We walked on them, joking of walking over tree-tops like giant epic heroes. They were tough, resilient, healthy trees, and they bore us no grudge for this childish play. We lifted one after another to a more appropriate tree-position to discover they were actually single trees, rooted at the ground, each elbowed eastward to follow the ground away from the prevailing wind. When we released them, they snapped vigorously back to their original position.

The reason for this strange tree-behavior, we came to understand, was the constant winds funnelling out of that deep valley from the west to apply a permanent, rock-like pressure on all growing things. If you were to be here and grow here, you would have to grow as that wind would permit. Up here, where life is chancy at best, negative-geotropism was just a nice theory. Survival—birthing, growing, living—was the primary principle. There was a vibrant urgency to things. The winds never stopped. They did warm and, I assume, gentle some with that warming. That was all there was. Whatever was to be done had to be done *now*, within the time span allotted between the snows.

This urgency was apparent in the flower structure. Flowers thrust their reproductive organs outward and upward in wildly sensual ways. They wasted no time in social convention, or energy on flowing petals. What energy they had, they expended all on a profusion of stamen and pistil. Plants were short, stubby, clustered together. That morning as we began our climb, I had seen asters a full two feet high, softly undulating with the wind in a small meadow at the base of the mountain. Here, at the ridge, these same species of aster were ¾ of an inch high—tough, stubby fellows looking all the world like those proverbial barroom fighters who never stay down no matter how often or how hard they are hit.

We lingered long on the ridge, sitting facing the west against that endless wind. What would we become were we to stay here forever? Would we have the tenacity—if we had the desire—to find the way to stay here? How much unrelenting resistance did we have in us to place against the unrelenting wind? What were our limits? It was obvious that ours were not as great as those limits of the permanent residents here, but then, we were not trees or mountain flowers. We were human beings and we could do other things and survive other places where these could not. That superiority seemed pitifully small here in their presence.

We left the ridge reluctantly, allowing just enough time to get to camp before dusk. Not much else was to happen, or could happen, that day. We met a buck deer in velvet, trying to use the path to go upward as we went downward. We jostled for position until he remembered a less travelled way and bounded off to take it. We rested beside an incredibly bubbly spring on the edge of the path, munching trail food and bits of cheese. The flowers were taller here, but in spite of their lusciousness, not nearly as beautiful as those stubborn, misshapen individuals of the same species up there on the saddle-ridge. I turned often to look back up to the horizon to save and savor the memory.

I had learned much of the limits of "elan vital" today. Never had

Asters, Continental Divide

If we are to be,
*   we must change.*
Nature knows
*   no other way but growth.*

life seemed so vibrant as it had there on that wind-punished ridge. Those who survived to birth and grow again had to be endowed with an incredible lust for life. They grew because they were *there* and that was all there was to it! Being there meant you had to hurry, not fuss about frills, adapt to what was at hand, and above all, be grateful for what WAS!

Many years later in the Wind River range in Wyoming, I climbed beyond the mountain meadows, beyond the glaciers to the rock-strewn peak where the full range of glaciered montains touched all horizons in the slanting western sun. This was indeed the mountain top from whence to touch creation's core. I saw ice storms forming and as they approached, huddled under their ferocity. Fog formed, swirled, slipped away to be sky again. Black, swirling clouds gathered about a peak and moved away like a crew of workmen making emergency repairs. Sudden gusts of wind raced up the advancing ridge, chilling, dampening. Gone, the air was warm again—even hot. Everything was primary, vital, basic.

This vitality exudes from them all—the mountain top, the mountain meadow, the glaciered slopes. Adder tongues blossom even as they melt their way through the perimeters of the receding snow-mass. Flowers root and grow in a layer of soil so thin it is unmeasurable. No spot is wasted. Something grows there. The moisture-laden soil is resilient, tough, adaptable. I walk carefully, reluctantly, stepping only because I cannot fly. I owe that bit of homage at least, for all around me I hear them say, "Live lustily, vibrantly, urgently! There is never enough time between the snows, so let there be pizzazz!"

Balanced Rock, The Arches

Weathered Juniper, The Arches

Mindpeeking

Mindpeeking
over horizons
where freedom romps,
heartsearching
the quiet places
where music swells,
I play the game of Seek.

By the rules,
ideas scamper,
hide in corners,
tease my mind,
and hover close.

By the rules,
I must search
behind the truths,
beyond the obvious,
and always find.

Park Place, The Arches National Park

Ashcroft, Colorado

Juniper, The Arches

Spider Rock, Canyon DeChelle, Arizona

In The Presence

Evening Shadows, Park Place, The Arches

Wonder
Is the only way
man can look at nature –
and survive.

Water Carrier

My maternal grandfather was a water-carrier. His endless trips with two pails of water fashioned a small Garden of Eden out of a barren prairie hilltop. Because of him, I tasted gooseberries, currants, horseradish, asparagus, rhubarb, long before I learned to like them. I climbed his apple trees, wondered at the strange names like quince, sour cherry, pear. His huge firs hid my red wagon during the weeks before my fourth Christmas—I know, I found it there!

Water-carriers have nurtured the earth with love and dependability. He was one of them. The arid South Dakota summers were rolled back by his determination to sponsor life and growth. In my most permanent mental picture of him, he is plodding across the north garden, two five-gallon pails of water in his hands, his head bent, his steps measured and steady. He seems like the one in charge of the earth, making it all happen.

I have a photograph of him holding me in his arms when I was a year old. He looks the way I remember him, but I wish I could remember the feel of him. It was a life-giving touch, gentling horses, events, trees. It must have been good for people, too. Sometimes I thought I could feel him in my mother—patient, dependable, loving, watering life as if it were a tree. Perhaps when we love all things that grow, it is good for people as well.

The Homestead, Ashcroft, Colorado

In The Presence

At the age of four, I learned to read on the kitchen floor in the house where I was born. I used wooden blocks, imagination, my parents and love. The experience still lives and grows. The coziness of the wooden floor, the delight of being in the wood box beside the big, black, imposing cookstove where my mother worked, creates a sense of presence, permanent and warming. She is always there and I am always near. Other memories become half-shadows, dimished by kitchen memories. Like springtime migrations, thoughts of life beginning and growing seem always to take me here and I am home.

A train carried me away. The sounds of a steam locomotive pulling into and out of a train station reverberate still in family memories. Fortified by idealism, youthful ignorance, the knowledge that I was loved, and with two days worth of fried chicken and homemade bread, I began my longest journey sitting on the new blue metal suitcase in the aisle of that crowded train. Not unlike newly hatched salmon fingerlings, I left my birth-home to discover who I could be. I am still on that journey.

Learning in school from a person was a new experience. Gone, the pseudo-fulfillment of high school requirements. Individual people— Dean Russell Olt, Carl Kardatzke, Adam Miller, Herb May, Clarence Hamilton, Walter Horton—embodied ideas, truths, thought processes. Like the cool water from the pump house I had just left, they refreshed my inner self. More than teachers, they sustained the tentative outreaches of mind and spirit, letting them become twigs, branches, trunks, supporting new growth. There, on the edge of aliveness with new friends, kitchen-memories matured into a life's work as full of love and warmth as that childhood woodbox. Sitting before these people re-birthed a childhood kitchen floor. Formation of word became formation of idea. Play gave way to a delightful life's

Teton Range, Wyoming

Bridal Veil Falls, Utah

work. Perhaps this is the greatest quest—to have life and love merge into one.

This was also a new land. Wide expanses of trees, endless streams of flowing water—so in contrast to the arid prairie—filled the landscape, demanding exploration. New people had new visions, new frontiers. At times overwhelmed, I explored new perimeters with them. Boyhood dreams were fulfilled—canoeing, hiking, building, exploring. A pioneer in my own life, I grew to admire the legendary courage, the will, the love of growth, that carried my ancestors from Norway to the barren plains of South Dakota. My own journey, though different, was no less exciting or perilous...how fortunate! Only hardship, difficulty, demanding challenges, can produce a life-legend. No one wants to settle for less. We only fear at times we must.

Retrospect glamorizes; but it also distills and a pattern emerges. Who we have been, and are, becomes the base for who we shall be. Growth alone survives.

One thing unfolds most clearly. To love is to be on the growing edge. Where our excitements are, our admirations, our courage to be open—there is where life is. Life "in the presence" is what Springtime is all about!

We must always leave.
It is the way
of growth.

Prairie Sunset

Alone

*Good thoughts
are windows,
opening out to life,
shattering
our aloneness.*

Shelter

49

To Live Again

The dove nest in the Russian olive did not survive the storm. The wind whipped the branches with such violence that now the nest lies tipped on the lawn, two cold lifeless infant bodies beneath. The dove returned almost before the storm was over, wings whistling as she dropped to the ground beside the nest. She waddled around it, head bobbing, absorbing the end of her dream. Finally, she rose to the branch where the nest had been, rested there for some time, then winged away.

Today, she and her mate are building a new nest in the young maple out front, their bodily functions re-ordered to accommodate again the cycle of fertilization, nesting, feeding. Some mysterious wisdom that cares for life and its progeny beyond the level of food and shelter helped them rise above tragedy to live again. Instinctive behavior, touching more closely the well-springs of ongoing life, seems now so superior to lives requiring decision, will-power. Being "in charge" of our life is at times an awesome burden.

Sagebrush, Arches

Real happiness comes
when we are able
to live what we believe,
rather than believe
what we are forced to live.

Always The Wind

I had forgotten about the wind. Now, standing outside my father's house, I remembered. Here on the prairie, there is always the wind. Its pressure is constant. During the dust storms of my childhood, it scoured the fields clean of topsoil and vegetation, buried fences, farm equipment and hope. We became so accustomed to it, we assumed it would never go away. It hasn't.

Strange, how good it felt. Almost forgotten were the hot, dry winds of August, the bitter, cold-driven winds of January, the raw, wet winds of March. Sheltered from their memory, my awe of them had receded. I stood reminded.

At nineteen, I exchanged these prairie winds for other wind-like pressures. These prairie winds had dramatized the necessities— shelter, food, warmth—making them precious. Newer winds of ambition, idealism, desire, had dramatized the need for life beyond the necessities. They were, in fact, the winds that blew me beyond my boyhood home. Thinking about this, I realized that it was life— not just the prairie—where there was always the wind.

On the elm west of the house, foraging barn swallows came and went, landing always to face into the wind. Only the sick, the defeated, turns its back on the wind. This knowledge is more difficult in the face of the winds of sorrow, of despair, or of loneliness.

The swallows cavorted in the wind, using its pressure to create rhythmical dances against the sun. Their grace, their delight in flight, exalted the wind, giving it positive, creative qualities. Watching their sleek, wind-carved bodies gave beauty to the wind-carved patterns on our own faces and lives. How much less we would be if there were not always the wind!

Icicles, Great Smokies

The Badlands, South Dakota

Remembering

Blackfoot Sundown, Browning, Montana

A Thing To Remember

It is early morning. I am rested and relaxed. The warming sun bathes my hand as I write. Pencil-shadows follow. So far today I have avoided arguments, the news of the day, any feeling of obligation, my own guilt about some nebulous thing and the weather reports. It is a sparkling feeling. Possibly, if I am very clever, it can last another one or two hours.

It will be a struggle, though, as it always is. The quality of incompleteness—whatever our age—dogs our every moment. Coming into being complete with all the appropriate accessories is reserved for automobiles.

One spring, after a particularly grueling period of work, I sought restoration in a solo camping, fishing trip on an island in northern Wisconsin. It was idyllic. A picture of the campsite could have graced the cover of any outdoor magazine. Open, shaded pine and birch woods surrounded a small clearing that sloped from a grassy level spot down to a crystal clear rock-fringed lake. Off to the right of the beached canoe, the lake became shallower, filled with lily pads and lined with reeds. That first night as the sun slipped down behind all this, casting a golden glow over everything, I knew true contentment.

It was an evening made for dreamy-eyed fishermen. Casting the bass lure among the lily pads was not fishing, it was an act of worship. I was ill-prepared for the excitement that followed, possibly because I had not yet learned that an atmosphere of serenity does not eliminate that fundamental predatory nature of all life. The life-death cycle is never interrupted, only at times, cloaked in gentler, less gruesome garb. Then, it is more easily accepted.

A boiling swirl churned the lake a good two feet away from the bass plug where it lay gently twitching in response to the rod tip.

My immediate thought was that this bass possessed incredibly poor aim to be able to miss by that margin. I twitched the lure in the most tantalizing manner I could imagine. It disappeared amidst a very business-like churn of water. I set the hook.

I had seen pictures like this many times—paintings of swarthy fishermen in red plaid shirts and lure-bedecked vests, pipe in mouth, skillfully handling the raging monster of the deep as it churned high into the sky in its futile freedom leap. I lacked the red plaid shirt, the pipe, the swarthy arm and, I am sure, the serene look of confidence. An enormous muskie rose out of the water as if catapaulted from the deep and tail-walked across the water to spray me with a shower of frenzied water. If he felt caught, I felt the more so. This was the golden moment of my fisherman fantasies, but the outcome was suddenly not so assured as I had assumed.

But we believe too much in the myths of things. In this case, that beautiful, full-length leap for freedom was almost all there was to it. A few short, dogged rushes and I beheld my prize alongside the canoe. He was enormous. I weighed five times his weight but felt five times smaller. Here obviously was my superior. What do I do now? I had only a small 10" bass net, no gaff and, more significantly, no experience. I felt the incredible urge to speak to my new acquaintance and say, "Please, may I?"

What followed was a comedy of errors and of a success that is the stuff of which legends and folk-lore are made. It is a story made for dying embers of campfires and for companions from whose eyes the flame of heroic adventure has not left.

As he lay full length in the water beside the canoe, undulating those enormous gills, I designed a course of action predicated, I am sure, on the illusion of his seeming friendliness. I was going to lay down the rod, and with my left hand slip the undersized bass net over his head as far as it would go, and then with my right hand, grasp his tail and hoist him into the canoe. I did this . . . almost all of it. The failure of this clever plan was due, I am now sure, to the fact that this muskie was super sensitive on his tail, for when I touched it, his departure was violently instantaneous. I was so stunned that I dropped the net—letting him race out into the lily pads with it primly set on his head.

Once more I coaxed him back to the canoe. We were almost friends by this time. He even let me untangle the net from his gills, from his teeth and from the two treble hooks of the bass plug. It was then that I noticed how nebulously he was hooked. One, almost straightened barb of one treble hook was wound into a single strand of slender mouth tissue hanging outside his mouth. That was all. His success—and mine—literally hung by that proverbial slender thread.

His wide gaping gills suggested a second chance at victory. I would slip my hand into his gills—gently—and then raise him out of the water in that traditional victory pose I had seen other fishermen do. I tried it. He was offended. He clamped his gills shut on my hand, headed for home again, this time scoring bloody ridges on both sides of my fingers as he left.

Possibly it was that, or possibly it was the fact of having a third chance at success, that so charged me with determination. When he was back full length alongside the canoe again, I plunged my hand so violently and with so much determination into his gills I almost thrust my hand up and out of his mouth. I had a firm grasp and I heaved upwards—this time with a real respect for the strength of my friend—and held him aloft. Why his airborne plunging and flopping didn't overturn the canoe, I am not sure, but I had my prize finally. He no longer had me. I strung a rope on him and in the now gathering darkness, led my raging warrior home.

Neither of us had been much of a success. He had lost, but I had lost too. I had lost all illusions of piscatorial prowess. I had not fished for muskie tonight, so his conquest was a total accident, and I never was to fish for muskie again. On other evenings I was to cast for bass again, but with a deeper humility. The spirit of my friend— all 37" of him—had established rather firmly the fact of my own frailty.

That story, being part of my own life-legend, has always warmed me—almost as much as this morning sun. Sometimes it appears as if someone had said, "Here, you need a 'thing to remember'," and gave it to me. However it came, I have my "thing" and writing of it is an incredibly delicious moment.

The world we see,
is the world
we carry with us.

The Horse Race

Quite probably it was the summer I was eleven that I saw the horserace. I remember I was small enough to be encouraged by the adults to stand in the front by the rope and yet old enough to understand a lot more about the race than just the winning or the losing.

It was the annual Fourth of July race held behind the rollerskating rink at Lake Campbell, South Dakota. The prize was twenty-five dollars. A local horse ridden by a tall, gangly boy I barely knew, was challenging a genuine Kentucky thoroughbred brought in by an outside promoter. The thoroughbred had a racing saddle and a bridle with those funny racing blinders on them. His rider had fancy clothes and shiny black boots and he carried a short whip. The local boy rode barebacked and barefooted. It isn't hard to imagine which horse we wanted to win.

My memory of the race consists largely of that golden moment when the horses pounded by me a scarce three feet away on the dirt road that was the track. My mental picture of this, however, is very vivid. The local horse and rider were next to me as they went by and I can still hear the gentle urgings of the rider as he lay almost flat along the neck of his horse, "C'mon, let's get 'im!" In that split second as they went by, and above all the straining of muscle and pounding of hoof, his voice came as clear to me as if there were no other sounds around. The horses were side by side with the local horse just a shade in the lead. I remember that too, because, unlike the good stories, he didn't win. It was only in that moment as he went by me that he was winning and that had to be my consolation.

It wasn't just local pride that made me notice the affection the boy and the horse had for each other. We farm boys knew a lot about the relationships between a man and a horse and this was a beautiful one. In that, our horse was far superior to the Kentucky thoroughbred. The thoroughbred had to be whipped every inch of the way—not just in the closing moments of the race. It was the quirt, not love, that made him run. His eyes told us that as he ran past.

Time has simplified the story for me, so that even though I've never told it before, it is a clear vignette of a noble way to live. It doesn't prove much, but it makes a lot of desperate winning at any price seem pathetically trivial.

Henri Dorval

Yesterday, high overhead, a wedge of Canadian geese made their way northward, their voices piercing the late March skies to authorize the Spring. I stood rooted in the stubble field, envying the purposeful beat of wing and voice driving them relentlessly to their nesting grounds.

In my mind's eye, I followed them: across the farmlands and the cities, the woods, the ponds and the big lakes — wondering which route they would take. Would they follow the shore lines of Huron and Superior to go inward to the west? Would they drive straight north to the shores of James and Hudson bays? or would they slant to the east over all those magic places whose names dramatized my boyhood reading: Nipissing, Timagami, Algonquin, Kipawa, Maskinonge? If they did, would Henri Dorval see and hear them? I visualized him laying aside his axe, his eyes searching skyward until he could follow their journey for a moment. I hoped that might happen. It would be a sentimental link across the miles and the years and would make the world a bit smaller and more personal.

Eric and I had caught his eye ourselves one late Spring on our journey north. We had slipped the canoe into the west bay of Ostabonigue Lake after a short portage from Lake Kipawa, when we heard his axe singing over the water. Eric, in the bow, saw the cabin—or rather the buff-colored Laborador—first. It was the dog that made us go closer. Eric wanted to see him better. Then it was Henri's voice, "I heard your paddles," that beached the canoe for us. It was mid-afternoon and we were searching for a ranger cabin we had been directed to, but it was warm and inviting to rest a bit in the sun.

Eric's friendship with the Laborador was instantaneous. Henri was pleased with that and launched into a tale of how the dog first came to him. "He came just like you, from over there. I heard him across the bay, barking and running along the shore. I took the boat and went to bring him here. He was so skinny and dirty and so hungry! No one has ever come to claim him and we like each other now. Are you as hungry as he was?"

We admitted we were hungry. "Well, stay for supper then, We can fish the walleye tonight and you can sleep good here. I have no work to do that cannot wait."

We stayed the day, the night, the day, and part of us has stayed forever on that point of land and Henri's cabin.

He was there to guide fishermen that came by plane from his brother's place to fish for a day or a week. During the winter, Henri stayed on to run a trap line over the ice-covered lakes—just because he wanted to be there. "I tried other things," he said, "but it wasn't any good. I wanted always to be here."

We rested, Eric playing with the dog as Henri finished chopping wood for the evening. Then he cleaned a big walleye for supper and started a fire in the wood cookstove. Such a meal! We who prided ouselves in our outdoor meals watched and ate in awe at this banquet in the north woods: French fries, slabs of Walleye deep-fried in huge skillets, homemade bread and hot, black tea. The meal was a celebration of life—and, as it turned out—of a friendship.

As darkness fell, we "fished the walleye"—Henri's way—with hand line, drifting over sand bars shoreward, rocking with the wind and the waves. Especially did he want Eric to catch a "good one." He tried so hard, but to no avail. We caught small ones, yes, but the "good one" eluded us.

That night, filled with stories and with food, Eric and I slept in a princely luxury that only friendship and warmth can bring. Our love for

Lake Superior Shore, Ontario

the woods and water matched his and cemented one of those friendships that requires no time or experiences for its existence.

The plane came the next morning, while Henri was improvising a landing net for that "good one" we were about to catch. The plane's burden, a solitary passenger, was so tipsy he had to be literally lifted out of the plane. As he staggered shoreward along the dock, he was muttering, "I'm gonna catch me the biggest damn fish'n the lake. Wheres the guy who's gonna he'p me?"

Henri became a different person—closed, brusque, remote. Out of respect to him in his newly acqured pain, we left to sleep the night at the ranger's cabin we had come to find.

When we returned the next morning to say good-bye as we had promised, Henri was relaxed again, his loathesome task completed. guess it was his disgust with the "sport" that helped most to understand our sudden friendship. When you love something the way we loved that country, you often mistakenly assume that it is a universal love, common to all who enter. Not so. Man is a predator. Often his predations are unsavory, calloused, destructive acts. Sated with food and comfort, he rapes and kills for the sake of his ego or his excitement. What Henri saw in us and we in him was a love for the world the way it was. We shared his joy in just being there. Such a friendship never dies.

It has been a long time and we've never been back, except in memory. The journey beyond his cabin was exciting, awesome and even dangerous, but our hearts stayed here. Somehow a common love always does that, fusing lives, building landmarks to shape another day.

Soul touches soul. The deepest in each of us responds to the common knowledge. If there is more to life than this mystic union of selves, I am unaware of it. Such experiences become mileposts more relevant than birthdays in the measurement of our lives.

Red Darner

Autumn's morning breeze, filled with cool nostalgia, whisked away summer's lazy notions. Cool winds of change energized both body and will, dispelling all thoughts of endless ease and lazy, sunny days. I walked in and out of sun, savoring the chill of shadow and the warmth of sunlight. My mind probed the meanings—if there were any—behind the passing of days and of seasons. Good times, like the sun, had been delightful to experience and even more delightful in memory. Then there were the dark times, shadowed moments when my will to achieve—or even survive—was so severely tested.

Notions of permanence teased their way into my dreams. If only things would not change so. But what moment or process would I immortalize? This nostalgic touch of Fall that makes the dreams of Spring all the more precious by their frailty, is only nature poised for another cycle. Surely this moment could not be the one...

With Those That Love

The Family

Sharing –
in any way –
warms and inspires
each of us.

The Cardinal Love Story

An incurable romantic can personify any object in nature, imbue purpose and whimsy to the most mundane event or process, and become sentimental over anything from old boards to seagulls soaring. I do not intend to change.

The Cardinal Love Story is one of the reasons. It occurred almost two years ago, but I think of it often, savoring both the fact and the delight of it. It is as important an ingredient in my search for being as any educational degree.

DISCOVERY

We found the cardinal nest in a low yew bush just eight feet outside the east window of the well-house. I removed that window, inserted a heavy cardboard with a hole in it for the camera lens. Inside the blind, I placed a platform on sawhorses for the camera tripod and a chair for me.

In a maple, some 50 feet the other side of the yew, the cardinal pair waited—anxious, nervous, wanting to get back to the nest. The male became increasingly active—flitting about, up, down, back and forth. He sang brightly, flicking his deep scarlet wings. Then—very ceremoniously—he rose into the air, flying in short, accentuated hops, singing all the while until he reached the maple close to me.

As he did this, I saw out of the corner of my eye that the female had dropped straight to the ground, and behind the protective cover of the yew, was hopping over the ground to the nest. She entered from the back, climbing up through the branches. Her tail flicked as she settled on the eggs.

I was unprepared for such coordinated intelligence. Awe-struck, I watched, camera inactive. His act of love that decoyed my gaze away from his beloved mate became a compelling preface to the "Cardinal Love Story" that was about to unfold.

FIRST DAY

The female left the nest when I entered the blind. Now she sat patiently hour after hour, beak open slightly, wings arched away from her body to dissipate her body heat made hotter by the sun. Occasionally she checked my presence, flinching when she first heard the camera. Everything is constant. She waits. I wait. Occasionally, the male will land on a branch nearby and call. She will cock her head to check his presence. He has not fed her while I have been here; perhaps he did so this morning.

I check photographic elements: habit patterns of the birds, direction of the sun, what pictures to take. I have three cameras, each with a different film and lens—one with motor drive. I need to bring another camera body.

The shadow of the well-house roof crept up towards the nest. When it crossed her tailfeathers, I left. She flew off, flicking her tail nervously. From a distance, I watched her return. She did not wait long.

SECOND DAY

I came into the blind from the back side when I returned. The female lifted briefly from the nest, perching hesitantly on the top branch, long enough for me to see that two eggs had hatched. One egg remained. She returned immediately.

On the nest, she was nervous, uncertain, intense. She lifted repeatedly, cocking her eye to look under her. Things were

69

happening there. Frequently she shifted feet—even standing spraddled on the edge of the nest for a moment.

Then the "Cardinal Love Story" unfolded with a flourish. First the male landed on a drooping branch of the maple immediately behind the yew. He had a small green worm in his beak, but sang brightly—even exuberantly. The female had seen his flight but now he was hidden from view. She craned her neck trying to see him. When she heard his song, she lifted from the nest, stretching her neck until she could see him through the branches and sang to him an obvious song of young motherhood. The happiness of the family fairly vibrated the air about them. As he entered the nest from behind, she lifted and the both of them looked under her, examining their young family. Then he held the green worm while she picked tiny bits to feed each of the young.

A few moments later, I heard him. From high up in an oak 200 yards down the road, he was singing all the cardinal songs he knew. Joy hath no other words but song!

THIRD DAY

Today, the third egg still had not hatched, but there was something wrong with one of the young. He was a dull yellow color. I touched him gently. He was cold. My first thought was to take him

70

from the nest, but some greater wisdom halted me with the thought, "This must happen often—how do the birds handle it?" I opted to wait and see.

The female returned. We both settled down to waiting, watching. Shortly, he called from somewhere I could not see. She lifted and flew off the nest to the right. Instantly, he appeared from the back, worm in beak. He minced the worm, dropped a portion into one raised mouth, turned to the other—now a cold, still body. He nudged it, holding the worm close to the head, "talking" constantly in a chuttering voice. He repeated the movement several times, cocking his head to look more closely. Finally, he gave up, fed the worm to the first bird, looking once more at the still form. When the female called, he left as she came in the back way.

For the remainder of the afternoon, he brought food every 9 to 11 minutes, both of them ignoring the still body in the nest.

I was more anxious than curious, I guess. What would they do with the dead body? When I looked, it was gone and the other egg had hatched. I scanned the ground under the nest. The body was not there. It had not been a matter of nudging it out onto the ground. Something considerably more formal had occurred. A decision had

FOURTH DAY

been made and carried out. Tragedy had been dealt with.

The new cardinal baby was, of course, smaller than the first. Time was to reveal it was also a female. Was that, too, a design of nature? It seemed then that it would be worth the time necessary to learn the truth of that hypothesis. We do spend our lives on lesser causes....

By now I was totally entwined in the lives of this young family. Everything else I was to do for the week became quite secondary. She came to accept me, too, allowing me to approach arm's length before threatening to fly. She would tense briefly until she recognized me, then settle back down. I was a "friend of the family." I honestly did feel honored, and looking back, I don't find that strange at all.

FIFTH DAY

It was getting to be work. The young mouths were always open. There was something about that, too. Every jiggling or jarring of the nest produced a pair of upstretched necks and open mouths. I used this automatic response to pose them for their "fifth-day portraits." Each day was a "My, how you have grown!" day.

Feeding was constant. I wondered about food supply. The male was still supplying it all. Today, he stumbled on a bumper crop of wood roaches. The diet had been green worms, caterpillars, moths and an occasional carpenter ant that the pair broke up carefully before feeding to the young. The wood roaches were another matter.

An adult wood roach is ¾" long, ¾" wide and thin enough to crawl under the bark of a log. They are 95% fibrous wings, tough, and—as the female cardinal found out—virtually uncrushable.

She tried her best! The male thought he had finally solved the world's food shortage—coming back with another even before she had succeeded in getting the first into a young mouth. The problem was that the roaches did not fit into 5-day-old mouths. They hung

over the edges and no amount of pushing, shoving, or re-arranging could get them far enough down to stay. She would get it partly in an open mouth and the roach would pop out the moment she released it. Back for more chomping and try again. Roaches do not mash. They resist dissection. The young became tired trying to hold their heads up, beaks open, and collapsed into the nest without eating.

She succeeded a few times, once almost strangling one baby with his so-called meal. The crisis finally came when the male brought a wood roach, size "XL". She tried—really tried. She chomped and chomped, occasionally stopping to meditate on the process. When she laid it across an upturned beak, it hung over the edges in all directions. She cocked her eye to see it better, surveying the problem. Then she picked it up, looked off into the distance as if trying to find a place to hide it—then ate it! It was such an act of parental frustration, I laughed out loud.

Now, I don't know how it was communicated, but I never saw another wood roach!

Both parents are feeding now. Sometimes they worked in relays, sometimes together. When the sun got hot, she straddled the young with her wings spread, shielding them from the sun. She seldom moved from this position during this time except to shift her feet when one of the young stirred. These were the tedious "years." The joy of new birth was over, the periods of first things past, the demands for food greater. Song gave way to simple chirps. The male, returning with food, had only to "chip" once and heads would emerge from under the female to eat and submerge again for shelter. The intervals between feedings grew shorter and his time at the nest briefer.

SIXTH DAY

Our Daily Bread

Family Portrait

Occasionally he would call a different call and she would slip off to catch a bit of food or drink for herself. On one occasion, he encountered a problem.

Having raised a family using diapers and flush toilets, I had never asked the question: Why are bird nests, after the young leave, so clean? I was to know both the question and the answer.

When he finished feeding the young, one of them dipped its head to lift his tail and expose a white feces sac. He reached over, pulled it out and prepared to fly away to drop it some distance from the nest. His hold on it was poor. He shifted it to get a better grip. In so doing, he squeezed a sizeable amount of feces out onto the back of one of the young. He saw it happen, cocking his head to look at the problem. He again thought of leaving, then re-examined the back of the young bird. He opted not to leave. He disposed of the remainder of the feces sac and proceeded to clean up his young baby. Gently and meticulously, he cleaned each pin feather, wiping it with his beak. The young bird squirmed and he talked to it in a low clucking voice as he worked. Several times he went over the back of that young bird, and it was only when he was completely satisfied that it was clean did

he stop to rest and wait for his mate to return.

Being a cardinal father isn't a bit easier than any other!

They almost fill the nest now. I sensed my vigil would soon end. Ornithologists predict ten days for the young in the nest and 2-3 weeks of parental feeding (largely by the male) after leaving the nest. This family was obviously preparing for that latter stage.

The parents did not remain with the young all the time. They fed as often as they found food, seldom resting. When they did rest, it was often near, rather than on, the nest. They often rested together as well.

SEVENTH DAY

In the blind, I had moments of impending loss. I wondered what I had missed, what had been my photographic inadequacies? I checked and re-checked. What else could I do before these golden moments would be gone forever?

I had photographed a lot and felt good about the results. One thing I had done more than any other, I had watched and learned. Time had been foreshortened and a lifetime of my own raising of children had been encapsulated into 8 days. Vicariously, I shared the tedium, the joy, the tension, the sorrow—re-examining my own parenting as I went. Like life itself, each day was too short. Time goes too fast.

EIGHTH DAY

The young male sat on the edge of the nest today, his colors starting to show on the tips of his feathers. The smaller female still kept to the safety of the inner nest, huddling down tightly when she saw me. But when he moved, so did she, humping herself up the wall of the nest to follow his lead. It was getting close. I had not much longer.

It was a cloudy day. I suddenly realized it was the first we had experienced. I waited for a few patches of sun, made a few exposures and left early. I still had two more days....

DEPARTURE

It is dangerous to believe the authorities on any subject. When I saw the young out of the nest, I assumed a tragedy. After all, this was only the ninth day, not the tenth!

My attempts at putting the young "back" were futile. It wasn't until after I had tried several times that I recognized a new call from the parents. I put the young back one more time and stood away. The call came and both of the young hopped from the nest to the branches of the yew. They were not very good at the art of branch-sitting. One by one they tumbled through the branches to the ground. The parents were on the grass beyond the yew, flitting about and calling, leading their children tumble-weed fashion over the grass to the safety of a long row of fitzers the other side of the lawn. I watched them until they were gone from view and from my life.

My throat was choked, my eyes wet. Good-byes are always painful. I was embarrassed, too, at my incredible human ignorance in harboring the notion that I was necessary in the scheme of cardinal lives. It came to me then, and even more so now, I needed them more than they needed me. I still do.

Swan Nesting

When Beauty Calls

That all things blossom,
   is nature's affirmation
   of the essential beauty
   of all things. Each living
   organism proclaims that
   the continuance of life is
   – in and of itself –
   a joyous feat.

Two –
is a
beautiful
number.

Brown-eyed Susans, The Smokies

Autumn Rose

Red-bellied Woodpecker

Hummingbird

Marsh Wren

Blue Jay

*The woods or the fields without the song
of birds would be a life without joy,
a day without sunshine. No silence would
be more devastating.*

Scarlet Tanager

Butterfly on Bergamot

Elegance At Dawn

Dandelioned

There are no ordinary things, only ordinary ways of seeing things. The camera constantly reminds me of that. The first time I really "saw" a dandelion, I was routinely photographing the "yellow" of dandelions, probing different perspectives, lightings, settings, backgrounds, relationships. I attached a bellows to the camera and moved in as close as the lens would focus. It was breathtaking! I stepped back from the viewfinder. It was not a trick. It was still the same dandelion! It seemed impossible . . . such wonder from the commonplace . . . .

I made exposure after exposure, first of the same dandelion and then of other dandelions. The wonder increased with their variety. I had "discovered" the dandelion! I must tell the world! Only the stark logic of necessity could ever make me mow the lawn again.

What if the blooms were bigger—several inches in diameter—so that the naked eye could see them better, would our respect for them increase? Or would that, too, become commonplace and wonder-less? Perhaps it is the act of discovery with its own sense of private possession that contains the joy. I am not sure. I only know that the experience has never left me and that my camera is a wiser instrument for having been "dandelioned." It expects to see more, and therefore it does!

Spring Reflections

The greening earth
  so alive
  so fresh
  so awake,
spins a tapestry of wonder
in my mind.

Wind-swirled leaves, like four o'clock students, explored the hidden
corners of the building, spiraling out through the barren trees,
spreading ecstacy in the branches and in me. Their ballet enthusiasm
and contagious energy, encouraged Winter's defection, leafing Spring
in me and all about. Green thoughts, chlorophylled images, softened
March's dull edges and spring-cleaned that dour thought. Recurring
dreams were born again in me. Remnants of living sprang to life,
sensualizing the barren places of my mind. A vibrancy, like the urge
to migrate, stirred in me. A restless belonging, stronger than any
calendar, proclaimed once again—SPRING IS HERE!

Sunflower

Spring Sunshine

*Nature's skill
is in making beauty –
not in preserving it.*

Leaf in Water, Jamaica

My path
   winds through a skittering of leaves
      randomly placed for me
         by the wind. How like
            the wanderings of my mind
               on the growing edge. . .

96